EL LIBRO DE
LAS PALOMITAS DE MAÍZ

Tomie de Paola

EL LIBRO DE LAS PALOMITAS DE MAÍZ

Traducido por Teresa Mlawer

Holiday House · New York

PARA FLORENCE NESCI,
quien me enseñó cómo hacer
las mejores palomitas de maíz
del mundo entero

Copyright © 1978 by Tomie de Paola
Translation copyright © 1993 by Holiday House, Inc.
All rights reserved
Printed in the United States of America
Library of Congress Cataloging-in-Publication Data
De Paola, Tomie.
[The popcorn book. Spanish]
El libro de las palomitas de maíz / Tomie de Paola ; traducido por
Teresa Mlawer.
p. cm.
Translation of: The popcorn book.
Summary: Presents a variety of facts about popcorn and includes
two recipes.
ISBN 0-8234-1058-7.—ISBN 0-8234-1059-5 (pbk.)
1. Popcorn—Juvenile literature. [1. Popcorn. 2. Spanish
language materials.] I. Title. 93-18318 CIP AC
TX799.D4617 1993

AQUÍ ESTÁ. . . .
"El maíz se conserva mejor en un pote cerrado, en el refrigerador, para que los granos conserven su humedad".
TONY, ¡ESTO ES MUY INTERESANTE! ESCUCHA. . . .

"Las palomitas de maíz fueron descubiertas por los indios de las Américas miles de años atrás".

"Cuando Colón llegó al Nuevo Mundo, una de las primeras cosas que observó fue a los indios de la isla de San Salvador, que vendían palomitas de maíz y las usaban como adorno".

PRIMERO, PONGO A CALENTAR LA CAZUELA.

"Pero en realidad, las palomitas de maíz son más antiguas todavía. En una cueva de murciélagos, en Nuevo México, unos arqueólogos encontraron palomitas que habían sido cocidas 5.600 años atrás".

"Y en Perú se encontraron granos de maíz de más de 1.000 años que todavía se conservaban en buen estado para hacer palomitas con ellos".

AHORA, EL ACEITE DE COCINAR.

"Los indios de las Américas conocían varias maneras de hacer palomitas de maíz. Una de ellas era sosteniendo la mazorca de maíz con una vara sobre el fuego".

"Pero de esta forma se perdían muchos granos".

"Otra manera era lanzar los granos directamente al fuego. Las palomitas saltaban por todas partes y el trabajo de recogerlas no era nada fácil".

BIEN. YA ESTÁ LO SUFICIENTEMENTE CALIENT[E] PARA ECHAR ALGUNOS GRANOS

"En 1612, exploradores franceses vieron a unos iroqueses haciendo palomitas de maíz en ollas de barro".

"Llenaban las ollas con arena muy caliente, echaban los granos de maíz y los revolvían con un palo".

"Una vez cocinado, el maíz saltaba encima de la arena y era fácil sacarlo".

"A los iroqueses les gustaba mucho la sopa de palomitas de maíz".

¿SOPA?

"Los algonquinos, quienes asistieron a la primera cena del Día de Acción de Gracias, obsequiaron a los peregrinos con palomitas de maíz".

"A los colonizadores les gustó tanto que desde entonces servían palomitas de maíz con crema de leche en el desayuno".

AQUÍ ESTÁ LO QUE LEÍ AL PRINCIPIO.

"El maíz se conserva mejor en un pote cerrado, en el refrigerador, para que los granos mantengan su humedad".

"Si los granos se resecan, quedarán muchas "solteronas" en el fondo de la cazuela. "Solteronas" son los granos que nunca llegan a convertirse en palomitas de maíz".

PARECE QUE NO HAY SUFICIENTE

"Si el maíz se seca demasiado, puedes agregar una o dos cucharadas de agua al pote y agitarlo hasta que el agua sea absorbida".

"Los granos de maíz estallan porque su centro es húmedo y pulposo, y está rodeado de una corteza dura de almidón".

"Cuando los granos se calientan, la humedad se convierte en vapor y el centro crece hasta que la corteza explota".

¿ESTÁS SEGURO DE QUE NO ECHASTE DEMASIADO MAÍZ EN LA CAZUELA?

NO DIGAS TONTERÍAS

"De acuerdo con una leyenda de los indios norteamericanos, dentro de cada grano de maíz vivía un pequeño demonio. Cuando su casa se calentaba, éste se ponía tan furioso que reventaba".

"Hay diferentes clases de maíz:
Los de granos blancos y amarillos son los que se encuentran más comunmente en los comercios".

"El más pequeño se conoce como 'fresa' porque sus granos son rojos y la mazorca parece como una fresa".

" 'El arco iris' tiene granos de color rojo, blanco, amarillo y azul. También se le conoce con el nombre de 'Calicó' ".

"También hay maíz de color negro, pero, no importa el color, las palomitas son siempre de color blanco".

"Los granos más grandes se conocen como 'Dinamita' o 'Copo de Nieve' ".

AGITA,
AGITA,
AGITA

"A la mayoría de las personas les gusta añadirle mantequilla derretida y sal a las palomitas de maíz".

"Si se agrega sal en la cazuela antes de que el maíz salte, éste se endurece.

AGITA, AGITA, AGITA

"Hay muchas historias sobre las palomitas de maíz. Una de las más conocidas y graciosas proviene del medio oeste de los Estados Unidos.

Un verano hacía tanto calor y la sequía era tan fuerte, que todo el maíz comenzó a saltar.

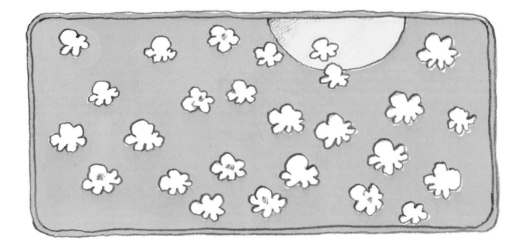

En un abrir y cerrar de ojos, el cielo se llenó de palomitas de maíz.

Parecía que había tal ventisca, que todo el mundo se puso sus mitones y sus bufandas y sacó las palas de nieve".

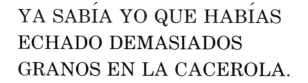

DOS FORMAS DELICIOSAS DE HACER
PALOMITAS DE MAÍZ*

PARA TODOS LOS DÍAS

1. Pon a calentar una cazuela mediana (con su tapa) a fuego alto por 2 minutos.
2. Agrega ¼ de taza de aceite de cocinar en la cazuela. Debe cubrir el fondo.
3. Baja la candela a fuego medio.
4. Echa 3 ó 4 granos de maíz.
5. Cuando comiencen a saltar, agrega suficientes granos para cubrir el fondo de la cazuela. (No eches más de ½ taza).
6. Baja la candela, cubre la cazuela y agítala.
7. Cuando el maíz ya no salte más, echa las palomitas en un recipiente hondo. Agrégale mantequilla derretida y sal.
8. ¡Para luego es tarde!

PARA EL VIERNES POR LA NOCHE

Receta de Florence Nesci.

1. Vierte aceite vegetal (como Crisco) en una sartén grande que tenga tapa.
2. Deja que el aceite se caliente a fuego lento.
3. Agrega suficientes granos para llenar el fondo de la sartén. El aceite debe cubrir los granos de maíz. Añade más si fuese necesario.
4. Revuelve constantemente hasta que 1 ó 2 granos comiencen a saltar. (Los granos se inflarán y se pondrán suaves).
5. Cubre la sartén, sube el fuego y muévela muy rápido hasta que el maíz no salte más.
6. Pon las palomitas de maíz en un recipiente hondo y échale sal. No es necesario ponerle mantequilla.
7. ¡Buen provecho!

Asegúrate de pedir permiso a un adulto primero.

SAL

Simon, Seymour.
  Ghosts.   Drawings by Stephen Gammell.   Lippincott
[c1976]

  79 p.   illus.   (The Eerie series)

  Nine supposedly true stories about ghosts and hauntings.

  1. Ghosts.   I. Title.

Other titles in THE EERIE SERIES

MOVIE MONSTERS
by Thomas G. Aylesworth

MEET THE WEREWOLF
by Georgess McHargue

GHOSTS

Seymour Simon

Drawings by Stephen Gammell

J. B. LIPPINCOTT COMPANY   **Philadelphia and New York**

Pictures appearing on page 12 courtesy of the French Embassy and Information Division, New York, New York; pages 29, 30 courtesy of *Newsday;* pages 42, 47 courtesy of Indre Shira; page 59 courtesy of D. Scott Rogo; page 74 courtesy of Culver Pictures, Inc.

U.S. Library of Congress Cataloging in Publication Data

Simon, Seymour.
  Ghosts.

  Includes index.
  CONTENTS: The noisy ghosts of Calvados Castle.—The nameless horror of Berkeley Square.—A Long Island spirit. [etc.]
    1. Ghosts—Juvenile literature. [1. Ghosts] I. Title.
  BF1461.S5   133.1   75-37520
  ISBN-0-397-31664-X   ISBN-0-397-31665-8 (pbk.)

For all my friends—
believers and nonbelievers

CONTENTS

INTRODUCING GHOSTS AND HAUNTINGS

Just what are ghosts and hauntings? To some who believe in such things, ghosts are the souls of dead people wandering among the living. Sometimes the ghosts are said to come back often. These ghostly visits are called hauntings. To nonbelievers, stories about ghosts are like fairy tales or folk legends. They are fun to listen to but difficult to believe in.

Ghosts seem to take many different forms. In the stories told about them, ghosts may look just like people. Other ghosts may look wispy or appear just as lights. Still other ghosts may come in shapes so frightening that they seem to have stepped out of a bad dream.

Some hauntings are made up mostly of noises, from mysterious footsteps to groans and cries to unexplained thumps and bangs. Other hauntings involve objects that move about. Sometimes people see the objects move, while other times the objects move only when no one is present.

Some ghosts seem to want to warn the living in some way. Others seem to be evil spirits and bring harm to the people that see them. Still other ghosts just appear and have nothing to do with the people who see them.

How do stories about ghosts and hauntings start? Someone will say that he knows a person who saw a ghost, and the ghost did this or that. Sometimes you even meet a person who will tell you that he actually saw a ghost and describe what it did. Of course, there is no way to check these stories. You can believe them or not, just as you like.

But some stories of ghosts or hauntings can be checked. There may be a number of people who say they saw the ghost. They may see the ghost at the same time or at different times. There may be photos of the ghost. And sometimes things happen which are difficult to explain unless you believe in ghosts.

Do all the stories about ghosts prove that they exist? Not really. At one time there were stories about how you would fall off if you came to the edge of the earth. Today we know that the earth is not flat and that you won't fall off. There were stories about dragons and flying horses. We know now that dragons and flying horses are not real.

There were also stories about flying ships and people going to the moon. But today there *are* flying ships. We call them airplanes. And people have gone to the moon. Sometimes stories turn out to be true and sometimes they don't.

Where does that leave us about ghosts? Simply that we don't know enough to explain every ghost story. Some ghost stories sound as if they were made up to scare us. Others just make us wonder. But some ghost stories have been checked into and sound as if there is something to them.

This book is a collection of different kinds of ghost stories. Some take place in this country in a house such as you or your friend might live in. Others take place in haunted castles or haunted graveyards. Some of the stories may be frightening. Others may puzzle you.

Many people enjoy reading about ghosts whether they believe in them or not. And that, finally, is the reason for this collection of ghost stories. It's not going to prove or disprove anything. It just may make you shiver a little bit and wonder . . . can such things be?

The Chateau de Falaise Calvados

THE NOISY GHOSTS
OF CALVADOS CASTLE

Calvados Castle is a gloomy-looking castle in France. It was built hundreds of years ago in the Middle Ages. Cold and damp, the castle hardly looks like a place in which anybody would want to live. If you saw it, you might think it was a perfect place for a ghost. And you would be right. Calvados Castle is haunted.

The first record of ghostly happenings came in 1875. The family and the servants that lived in the castle were disturbed night after night by mysterious sounds. They decided to place threads across the open doors. They hoped that the threads would be broken so that they could learn where the intruders came in. The sounds continued, but the threads were never broken.

The owner began keeping a diary of the strange events. The diary tells that on the night of October

13, 1875, a teacher employed by the family was alone in his room. All of a sudden he heard a series of raps on the wall. He saw the candlestick moving by itself on the mantelpiece.

Terrified, the teacher called the owner of the castle. The owner came into the room and examined it closely. He found that a chair which had been tightly bound down to the floor had moved toward the fireplace.

For the next two days loud poundings on the castle walls continued. The owner of the castle armed himself and went in search of the noisemakers. But he found nothing. He heard only the sound of ghostly footsteps.

For a few days the poundings on the wall and other noises stopped. But it was only a short rest. On October 31 the castle was filled with ghostly sounds and noises.

The owner wrote in his diary of that disturbed night. He said that the noises sounded as if someone were running up the stairs with superhuman speed, stamping his feet. When the loud steps reached the first floor landing, there were five heavy blows on the walls. Then it seemed as if a heavy log were thrown against the wall. The house shook with the blow.

Everybody ran out on the landing to see what had made the sounds. But they found nothing. Returning to their rooms, they heard the noises beginning once again. The noises stopped only at three o'clock in the morning. Finally the family fell into an exhausted sleep.

The next night the weird noises continued. This time everyone was awakened by the sound of a body rolling down the stairway. When it finally thumped to the bottom of the stairs, something seemed to pound wildly on the walls.

Night after night the sounds continued. Loud blows rocked the castle's walls. Ghostly footsteps ran from one place to another. The family and the servants were terrified. In his diary the owner described the footsteps as having nothing human about them. He wrote that they sounded like two legs without feet, walking on the stumps.

By the middle of November the ghosts seemed to be even more threatening. So far there had been only thumpings. But now there began wild screams and noises. There were long shrieks, one after another. It sounded as if a woman were crying for help.

The cries filled the entire castle. Screams, moans, groans, and all kinds of unearthly sounds echoed

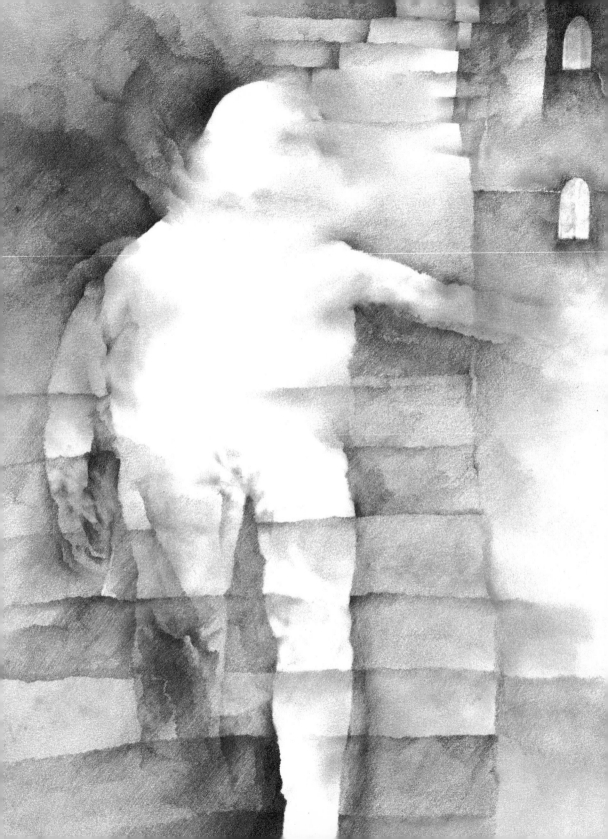

through the halls and the cellars. The sounds frightened the listeners. The owner wrote that they sounded like the cries of demons or the damned.

Not only was the castle filled with noises, but the furniture suddenly began to move. Beds overturned by themselves. Windows were flung open. Chairs shifted from one place to another. The family's Bibles were torn to shreds.

There were even attacks on people. The owner's wife went to the door of a room from which noises were coming. She put out her hand to open the door. Before she could touch the door, she saw the key turn quickly in the lock. It flew out and hit her left hand. The blow was so strong that her hand turned black and blue.

The following months brought no relief, only new and more horrible sounds. There were shrieks like a bull roaring. Every floor shook with hammerings. It sounded as if cattle were stampeding through the halls. Crazy laughter was the final terrifying touch.

The family called in a priest to get rid of the ghosts. They placed religious objects all around the castle. The noises seemed to stop for a while. But not for long.

One morning the family found that all the religious objects around the castle had vanished. A few days later the objects fell on a small desk where the owner's wife was writing. After this the blows and noises started once again.

We do not know what finally happened a hundred years ago to the noisy ghosts of Calvados Castle. There is no record of whether peace ever came to the family living in that terrible place.

THE NAMELESS HORROR
OF BERKELEY SQUARE

In the 1890s the city of London seemed to be filled with houses said to be haunted. Perhaps the most famous haunted house in London was at No. 50 Berkeley Square. Berkeley Square was in an area of well-kept townhouses. But No. 50 stood out from the rest. It was unpainted, with rotting wood sides and rusty railings. Its broken windows gave it a sightless, haunted appearance. Crowds of visitors came to gaze at its run-down front and shiver at its frightening legends.

All kinds of stories were told about the house. One story was printed in the May 10, 1879, issue of a magazine called *Mayfair*. It states: "The house in Berkeley Square contains at least one room of which the atmosphere is supernaturally fatal to mind and body alike. A girl saw, heard and felt such horror in it that she went mad, and never recovered sanity

The haunted
house at
No. 50 Berkeley
Square

enough to tell how or why. . . . The very walls of the house, when touched, are found saturated with electric horror."

There were reports of several different ghosts that inhabited the house. One was the ghost of a child dressed in Scottish plaid. The child was supposed to have been frightened to death in the nursery. Another was the spirit of a young man said to have gone mad waiting for some message which never came. Still another was the ghost of a young lady named Adeline. She was said to have flung herself out of a top-story window.

But these were tame stories compared to that of the Nameless Horror. Newspaper reports of the time give two different accounts of what the thing looked like. One story said the Horror was a ghost in the shape of a man. But its face was unspeakably horrible—white and soft, with a great round hole for a mouth. The other story described the Horror as a creature with many legs or tentacles. It was supposed to have come out of one of London's ancient sewers.

There are several different stories of meetings with the Horror. The best known concerns two sailors in the British navy. One of the sailors later gave a complete report of his experiences to the police.

It seems that the two sailors found themselves in London without money. It was a cold, foggy day during the Christmas season. Passing by the deserted front of No. 50, they saw that the place was empty. They decided that they would take shelter there for the night.

They must have used candles to show them the way up to the bedroom. You can imagine the frightening shadows that the yellow flames cast against the walls. The sailors started a fire in the fireplace, using some strips of wood they found in the room. Getting into bed, they finally fell asleep.

The fire was still burning when they both awoke. Outside the bedroom door they heard the sound of footsteps. They were coming up the stairs. But they did not sound like the footsteps of anything human. They sounded like the padded steps of some large jungle animal.

Then the sailors saw something that was not human—or animal—pass through the wood of the closed door. In an instant they leaped out of bed and dashed toward the window. There they had placed some sticks for the fire. One sailor grabbed a stick and held it ready for use as a club.

But between them and the door stood the creature. Its claws were outstretched toward them. Its

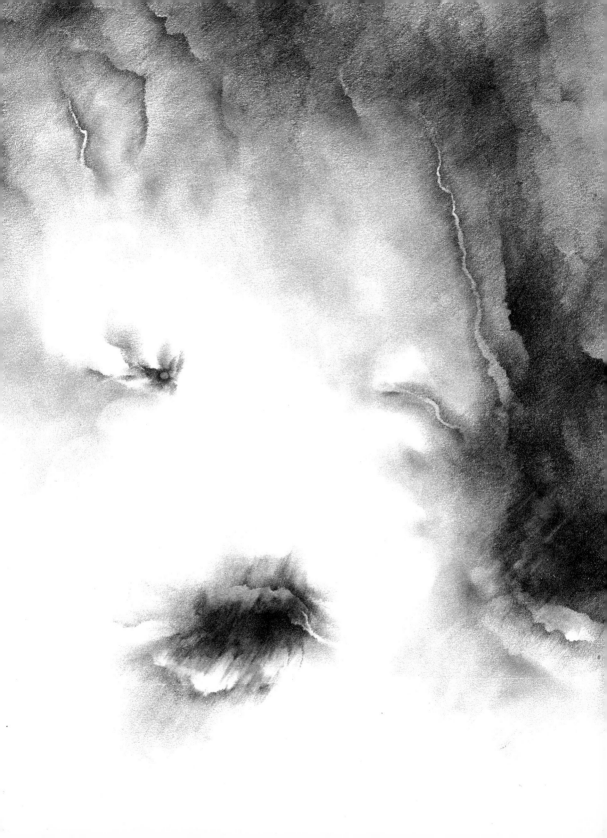

face was in shadow, and they could not make it out. It stood for a moment near the door. Then it began to move toward them. It panted and shuffled across the room. Its claws made scratchy sounds on the bare wooden floor.

As if it had decided on its victim, the thing sprang upon the sailor holding the stick. The sailor fell backward against the window. Part of the framework and the glass panes broke outward. The sailor screamed again and again.

The other sailor took this chance to escape. He sprang past the creature and dashed down the stairs. Behind him he heard scream after scream. He dashed out of the house and fell fainting upon the stone steps. Shortly after that he was found by a police patrol.

The police entered the house and went up the stairs to the bedroom. But the other sailor was not there. The window frame was smashed outward. In the yard below the police found the dead sailor with his neck broken. It was said that his wide-open eyes were filled with terror.

A few years after this story the empty house was rented to the family of a Mr. Bentley. For several weeks after moving in, the Bentleys noticed nothing odd. But then the younger daughter said that the place gave her the creeps. She complained that night after night she felt something was outside her bedroom door. And there was a peculiar smell, she said, like the odor of the animal cages in the zoo. Once she had even heard something sniffing and scratching at her locked door.

Because of this the family decided to invite the elder daughter's boyfriend to stay in the house. His name was Captain Kentfield. The night before his arrival a maid was putting his room in order. Suddenly everybody in the house heard her loud screams. They raced to the room and found the girl in a state of collapse on the floor.

They rushed the girl to the hospital. But she died the following morning. She never was able to explain what had happened. The only words the doctors heard her speak were, "Don't let it touch me."

Meanwhile Captain Kentfield had arrived at No. 50. He was told of what had happened to the maid. But Kentfield said that the idea of a ghost was just nonsense. He didn't believe one word of it. And he decided to sleep in the haunted room, even though the family was much against it. "I'll ring if I need help," he assured them.

Downstairs, the family gathered together in the dining room. One of their guests was a doctor. They decided that they would not sleep until they were certain that all was well with Captain Kentfield. A few minutes after midnight they heard his bell begin to ring loudly. While the bell was still ringing, there came the sound of a shot.

Mr. Bentley and the doctor raced up the stairs. They burst into the room. The young officer was lying on the floor. Some of the bedsheets were clutched in his hands. An army pistol lay next to his body. His face was a mask of terror.

The doctor quickly examined him. There was no sign of a wound. As far as he could make out, Captain Kentfield had died of a heart attack. But what had the captain seen that he had fired upon? What had made him ring the bell so loudly? There was nothing in the room, and no way to tell. But there were those who would say that the Nameless Horror at No. 50 had claimed still another victim.

A LONG ISLAND SPIRIT

Reports of ghosts are not always from long ago and far away. Every so often the daily newspapers will print a story about some strange happenings that don't seem to have a natural explanation. Usually the reporter will make fun of them and write the story in a humorous way. But the strange events may not be much fun to the people who are involved.

Here is the story of some well-reported events that took place during five weeks in 1958. They happened in the Seaford, Long Island, home of Mr. and Mrs. James Herrmann and their two children. The disturbances started on February 3 at about three thirty P.M., when Mrs. Herrmann was at home with her two children. They were her daughter Lucille, thirteen years old, and her son Jimmy, twelve.

The family first heard noises that sounded like bottles popping their caps. When they checked, they found a small bottle of holy water on Mrs. Herrmann's dresser lying on its side. Its cap was unscrewed, and all the water in it had spilled. In Jimmy's room they found a small ceramic doll. Its legs were broken. Next to it was a broken plastic model of a ship. In the kitchen there was an opened bottle of starch under the sink. Its contents had spilled. A bottle of bleach in the cellar had also spilled.

Other bottles were opened and spilled on the next two days, February 6 and 7. But it was only on the ninth that the family decided to call in the police. Things seemed to be getting out of hand.

On Sunday morning, February 9, the family was all in the dining room. They heard noises coming from different rooms in the house. They rushed to see what had happened. They found many more bottles opened and spilled.

The holy water bottle on the dresser had opened again and spilled. A new bottle of perfume on another dresser had fallen to the floor. It had lost its screw cap and rubber stopper and spilled. A bottle of shampoo and a bottle of Kaopectate in the bathroom had lost their caps and fallen over and were spilling. The starch in the kitchen was open

Jimmy Herrmann, surrounded by the types of bottles that popped open during the poltergeist activity in his home

and spilling. A can of paint thinner in the cellar had opened and fallen to the floor and was spilling.

These events disturbed the family so much that they called in the police. Patrolman J. Hughes of the Seventh Precinct came to the house. The family told him that they had felt no shakings of the house and heard no loud noises. In fact, there were no disturbances of any kind that might result in the bottles being knocked down. Patrolman Hughes heard a

29

noise and went into the bathroom to check. He found that the medicine and the shampoo had spilled again.

Later, other people saw objects moving around. A cousin of Mr. Herrmann was visiting the house on Saturday, February 15. She was seated in the living room with Jimmy and Lucille. Suddenly a small statue on an endtable began to move about. It flew two feet into the room and landed on the rug. Nobody in the room could explain what had caused the statue to move.

James Herrmann points to a dish, held by Mrs. Herrmann, that flew through the air in his house. The dish knocked off a part of the wooden cabinet behind him.

The same object moved on other days. For a second and even a third time the statue fell about two feet into the room. It did not break any of these times. But the fourth time it moved, it flew into a wooden desk about ten feet away. It shattered into bits.

These strange events troubled and upset the family. Mrs. Herrmann tried placing bottles filled with holy water around the house. But these were no help. In fact, they may have made matters worse. Many of the holy water bottles would lose their screw tops with an explosive sound, fall over, and spill.

Nothing could be found in them to explain why the tops should pop off. Five of the bottles were examined by a police laboratory. There was no suspicious material in any of them. The police were not able to come up with an explanation.

The house was checked and rechecked. Nobody could come up with a natural explanation for the movements. The Long Island Lighting Company placed an instrument in the ceiling. They wanted to see if the house shook during the incidents. They also carefully checked all the electric wires and lights in the house. They found nothing.

A cap was placed over the chimney. It prevented

any wind from coming into the house. Perhaps a down draft of wind from the chimney moved the bottles. The cap did no good. The Building Department came in and looked over the house. They found it to be in good shape. The Fire Department checked a well in front of the house. They found the water level had been the same for five years. A flooded basement did not move the bottles.

There was a meeting at Adelphi College at which members of the different science departments talked about the strange events. They also made visits to the house. They found no answers.

Two people from Duke University were present in the house when some objects moved. They were convinced that the movements were real. They thought that there was no trickery involved.

A total of sixty-seven different unexplained happenings was reported in the Herrmann house. Three of these were thumping sounds. The rest were movements of objects. On March 10 a bleach bottle popped in the cellar, lost its cap, and fell over. This was to be the last unexplained event.

During all these weeks the family was quite upset. They often went and stayed with relatives during this time. They wanted to get out of their house and away from the happenings. Finally, they came to see the problem as one for science. They felt that the happenings, while strange and disturbing, would eventually be explained. But to this day no one has been able to explain them.

THE RESTLESS COFFINS

The peaceful tropical island of Barbados in the Caribbean Sea seems to be an unlikely place for a ghost. Yet one of the most carefully investigated ghost mysteries of all time occurred on the island. No solution to the mystery has ever been found. To this day it remains a puzzle.

High on a hill overlooking Oistin's Bay in Barbados there is a small church. In the cemetery next to the church is a tomb. The tomb is built of large stone blocks solidly cemented together. It is sunken into the solid limestone rock of the hill. Its door was once sealed with a large slab of blue marble. It took several men to move the marble slab whenever the tomb received another coffin.

The tomb was built in 1724. Nothing odd happened in it till a wealthy island family named Chase bought it in 1808. The first Chase to be buried there was the infant daughter of Thomas Chase. The child was placed in a lead coffin. The coffin was brought to the tomb in February, 1808. The only other coffin in the tomb was a wooden one. It contained a Mrs. Goddard, buried there in 1807.

A few months later, in July, another daughter of Thomas Chase died. She was also placed in a lead coffin and buried in the tomb. Nothing was disturbed.

Four years later Thomas Chase died. The tomb was opened on August 9, 1812, to receive his body. The marble slab at the door was moved aside. The burial party went within. What they saw struck them with wonder. The lead coffins of Chase's two daughters were standing on end, upside down, at the far end of the tomb. The wooden coffin containing the remains of Mrs. Goddard was still in place.

The tomb was examined carefully. Nothing was found that could account for the movement of the two coffins. The burial party replaced the children's coffins beside that of Mrs. Goddard. Chase's heavy, lead-lined coffin was carried in by eight men. It was placed on the floor of the tomb. The door slab was replaced and cemented around the edges. Finally the stonemason placed his seal in the cement.

Four more years went by. In September, 1816, the

coffin of infant Samuel Brewster Ames was brought to the tomb. The cement was chipped away. The stone slab was removed from the door. The mourners looked inside. Except for Mrs. Goddard's, all of the coffins were scattered about the tomb upside down.

No one knew what had happened. They tapped on all the walls of the tomb. They found no break in any of them. Finally they replaced the coffins. They sealed up the tomb once again with cement.

Just two months later the tomb had to be reopened. The adult Samuel Brewster, a relative of the Chase family, had been killed in a slave uprising. He had been buried someplace else. Now his body was to be placed in the family tomb.

You can imagine with what dread the burial party viewed the tomb. The men chipped the cement away from the edges of the stone slab. The slab was drawn aside. The family looked within. The coffins were scattered about the tomb once again. Some were propped against the walls, on top of each other. Only the remains of Mrs. Goddard were not disturbed. Her wooden coffin had rotted away.

The lead coffins were returned to their places. Mrs. Goddard's remains were wrapped up and

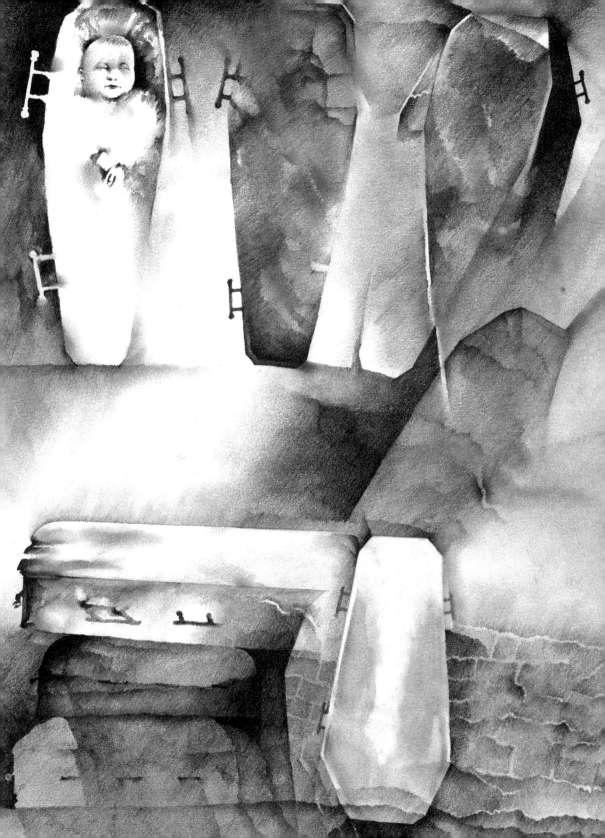

placed against a wall. Once again the tomb was examined, and nothing was found. The burial party withdrew. The tomb was carefully resealed.

The events in the tomb greatly excited the people of Barbados. The story became known all over the island. The tomb had to be reopened three years later, in July, 1819, when another family member died. The governor of the island, Lord Combermere, decided to attend the funeral.

The entrance rock was drawn back. The same scene of disturbance greeted the governor's eyes. The heavy coffin of Thomas Chase stood against a wall. The other coffins were scattered about.

The new coffin was brought in. All six coffins were arranged. The three adults' coffins were placed upon the floor. The three infants' coffins were placed atop them. Fine sand was scattered around the tomb to show footprints if anyone entered. The entrance slab was replaced and cemented. The governor placed his seal in the cement in the presence of witnesses.

The next episode took place on April 18, 1820. Here is the report of Sir Robert Schomburgh, writing in his book *The History of Barbados,* published in 1844.

"Lord Combermere was [living] in 1820 in the neighborhood of the church, and, having been told of this mysterious circumstance, he [asked] the Rector to have the vault reopened, when, to the astonishment of all present, the coffins . . . were found scattered about, and one of the largest thrown on its side across the passage, so that, had the door not opened outward, an entrance could not have been [made] except by removing the slab on the top, which is of immense weight."

None of the seals had been disturbed, and no footprints were found in the sand. The family was so upset at these happenings that they removed the coffins from the tomb. They had them buried in the churchyard. The tomb was filled in and closed.

That was the end of the incidents, but not the end of the mystery. What could be the explanation for the moving coffins? The seals that were still in place and the lack of any sign of entry seem to rule out human hands.

Only two "natural" explanations have been given. One says that earthquakes were the cause of the movements. But the idea that an earthquake could be confined to a small tomb and felt nowhere else on an island is harder to believe in than ghosts.

Another idea is that floodwaters floated the coffins about. But no watermarks were found. The tomb is at the top of a hill, an unlikely place for a flood. Nathan Lucas, a witness to the opening of the tomb in 1820, writes, "There was no vestige of water to be discovered in the vault: no marks where it had been, and the vault is in a level churchyard . . ."

The single clue to the mystery is that the Chase family coffins were the only ones moved. Had the family in some way wronged a human or ghostly force? We do not know the answer and will probably never know just what caused the restless coffins of Barbados to move.

THE BROWN LADY
OF RAYNHAM HALL

There are many tales of dimly seen figures walking about the halls of old houses. But this ghostly visitor is something special. You see, there is an actual photograph of her. It is reprinted on page 47. The photo was not the first appearance of the lady in brown. That dates back to many years earlier.

In 1835 there were many guests for the Christmas season at Raynham Hall, in Norfolk, England. The hosts were Lord and Lady Charles Townshend. Their guests included a relative, Colonel Loftus.

After dinner one evening Colonel Loftus settled down for a game of chess with another guest, a man called Hawkins. The game was a long, closely fought contest. It lasted till well after midnight. When the tired players went upstairs to go to their bedrooms, Hawkins noticed a woman standing by Lady Townshend's door. He thought the woman was dressed

Raynham Hall

very strangely, and pointed her out to his companion.

By the time the colonel had adjusted his eyeglass to get a better look, the figure was walking away down the hall. As they watched, the figure gradually faded from view.

Later that week Colonel Loftus saw the woman again. This time he quickly ran after her. He took a shortcut so that they came face to face on the staircase. In front of him was the ghostly figure of a woman dressed in a brown satin dress. The woman's face was lit up with a kind of unearthly light.

But it was another feature that shocked the colonel and made his face turn pale. The lady in brown had no eyes. Her eye sockets stared empty and black. By the time Colonel Loftus had gotten over his shock, the figure had disappeared.

Afterward Colonel Loftus drew a sketch of the ghost. Nobody laughed at him when he told them about his encounter and showed the sketch. The family told him that the ghost had been seen a number of times before 1835. Lord Townshend even said that he had seen the ghost go into his room just the previous night.

The next appearance of the ghost came a number of years later. There was a big party in Raynham Hall. Among the guests was Captain Frederick Marryat, an author of sea stories.

Marryat asked if he could sleep in the so-called haunted room. He told Lord Townshend that he thought the ghost stories were just nonsense. He was given permission. In the room hung a portrait of the brown lady that an artist had painted from Colonel

Loftus's sketch. As Marryat undressed for the night, he inspected the portrait. Was it his imagination, or was there a terrible touch of evil in that face?

Captain Marryat had almost finished undressing when two young men came to his room. They wanted to discuss the next day's hunting. When the men asked Marryat to come to their room to look at a new gun, he went at once. Since the other guests were asleep by now, he went as he was, in his underwear.

After a time they finished their discussion and started to walk back to Marryat's room, bringing the gun with them. As they were walking along the hallway, all three saw the figure of a woman approaching. Worried about his state of undress, Captain Marryat hid with his companions behind the door of a vacant room. As he looked at the figure, Marryat felt his hair stand on end. Coming toward them was the woman whose portrait was hanging in his room.

Without making a sound, the figure moved across the oak flooring. In her hand was a lamp which reflected on the brown dress she wore. As she passed the door behind which they were hiding, the figure turned her sightless face toward them with a horrible expression.

We can be sure that Captain Marryat was convinced that he was looking at an evil ghost, or something not human. Marryat pointed the hunting rifle he was carrying at the figure and fired point blank. The rifle bullets passed through the lady in brown, burying themselves in the door of a room across the way. The figure continued on down the hall.

For many years the ghostly figure was not seen again. But in 1926 it reappeared. Lady Townshend told a newspaper reporter that her son and a friend of his had met the lady in brown. They had seen her on the same staircase where she had been seen many years before. Neither her son nor his friend knew at the time they saw the figure that the spot was supposed to be haunted.

Ten years later came the most sensational evidence of all. On September 19, 1936, Mr. Indre Shira, a photographer, arrived at Raynham Hall. He was going to take a series of photographs of the house.

At four o'clock that afternoon, Shira and a helper named Captain Provand were getting some shots of the old staircase. Captain Provand had just taken a flashbulb photo of the staircase. He was placing a new photographic plate in the camera. Shira was standing behind him so that he could get a clear view of the bottom flight of stairs. Suddenly Shira saw a shadowy figure. It looked like a woman draped in a veil.

The figure started to float slowly down the steps toward the photographers. Shira yelled at Provand to make another exposure right away. In an instant Provand was ready. Shira fired the flashgun. The photograph was taken.

Provand, who had not seen the figure, asked what all the fuss was about. Shira replied that he had seen a ghostly figure gliding down the staircase. He said that he could see the steps through the figure.

Provand laughed at this. A ghostly figure? What nonsense! But Shira was convinced that he had seen something. In fact, he was so sure of what he had seen that he bet Provand that the photograph would show something unusual. And so it did.

When the photograph was developed, the shadowy form of a hooded figure of a woman could be seen. The picture was published in the magazine *Country Life* on December 16, 1936. The negative of the picture remains in the files of the magazine. Experts who examined the photographic film at the time were convinced that there had been no faking.

Look at the reproduction of the photograph carefully. Are you looking at a picture of a ghost? Or is it just a trick of the light? What do you think?

THE GHOSTLY HITCHHIKERS

Many different stories are told in America about ghostly hitchhikers. Some date back to the time of the horse and buggy. Others are modern, and the hitchhiker is given a lift in a car or a truck. It is almost impossible to track down the actual names of the people involved. Here are two of these stories.

The first story takes place in the 1930s in upstate New York around Binghamton. At that time there was a bad curve on a highway, Route 17. The curve, known as the Devil's Elbow, was often the scene of car accidents.

One night in October the weather was very bad. A cold rain had been falling for hours. There were few cars on the highway, and those that were moving crept along very slowly.

In one of the slow-moving cars a young book salesman strained his eyes as he peered through the rain-drenched windshield. He could barely make out the side of the road, even with his headlights on full. He knew that a few miles farther on was the Devil's Elbow, so he was extra careful.

When the salesman first saw the figure by the side of the road, he wasn't sure that it was a human being. But as his car moved closer, he saw a young woman standing in the rain. She was wearing a white coat and had a scarf over her head.

Although she did not signal him, the salesman felt that he had to stop. He pulled up his car alongside her, rolled down the window, and asked if she would like a lift. In a low voice she thanked him and got into the seat beside him.

The salesman asked her where she was going. She gave him an address a few miles ahead, just off Route 17. He could see that she was shivering with cold, so he offered her his jacket. She thanked him and slipped it over her shoulders.

The rain was coming down harder now. The salesman was paying close attention to his driving. The girl did not speak to him as he drove, and he nearly forgot that she was there. He remembered just in time when the turnoff came on the highway. As he drove up to the address that he had been given, he glanced over at the girl. But she wasn't there.

He stopped the car in amazement. He looked in

the back seat. Nobody there. Not only was the girl gone, but his jacket was missing, too. How had she gotten out? He hadn't stopped at any point along the way. He hadn't heard the car door open or close. He couldn't figure it out.

If his jacket hadn't been missing, and if there hadn't been a little pool of water in the seat where the girl had been sitting, the salesman would have begun to doubt his own senses. In any event, he was determined to get his jacket back.

The salesman climbed out of the car and went up to the old weathered house. He rang the bell once, then after a few minutes once again. Finally he heard footsteps coming to the door.

The door was opened by a woman in a flannel bathrobe. The salesman said he was sorry that he had awakened her. He said that as he was driving on Route 17, he had seen this young girl dressed in white and had given her a lift. She had given him this address, and . . .

"You don't need to go on, young man, I know what's happened. You see, it's my daughter. She gets restless at night when it rains like this. She wants to come home again. You understand that it was ten years ago that she was killed in a crash at the Devil's Elbow."

Stunned, the man went back toward his car. Could this really be? He got into the driver's seat and saw something on the seat next to him. It was his jacket, wet with rain.

Another story about a ghostly hitchhiker takes place in South Carolina. One night a man and his wife were driving toward the city of Columbia along a lonely stretch of highway. On each side of the road was a steep drop of fifteen feet to a ditch. Beyond the ditches lay a swamp.

The headlights of the couple's car picked out the figure of a girl walking along the road. She was well dressed and carried a travel bag in her hand. They slowed their car to a stop to see if she wanted a lift at this late hour.

The girl thanked them and got into the car. Since the car was a two-door sedan, the wife held the back of her own seat forward so that the girl could get into the back seat. The girl told them that she was going to visit her mother in Columbia, who was seriously ill. She gave them the address of the house.

The couple talked together in the front of the car. After a while the wife turned around to ask the girl in the back whether she would mind if they stopped off for some coffee. But there was no answer. The girl had vanished.

The frightened couple didn't know what to do. There was no way the girl could have left the car from the back seat without their knowing it. Finally they decided that they would go to the address the girl had given.

It was late when the man and his wife reached the house. The windows were dark, and there seemed to be no one awake. They decided to ring the bell anyway. After waiting for several minutes, they saw a light go on in an upstairs bedroom and heard footsteps coming to the door.

The door was opened by a sleepy-looking young man. As they began to tell him the story of why they had come to the house, he interrupted them. "You needn't go on. I know the rest of the story. The young lady was my sister. She was killed in an automobile wreck on the highway through the swamp three years ago. She had been on the way to the hospital to see our mother. Two other people have come here in previous years to tell of the same experience you just had. And each time it was on the same date, the anniversary of her death."

THE S.S. *WATERTOWN* PHANTOMS

From ships and planes disappearing to sightings of ghostly sailing ships and strange sea creatures, the sea has always been a place where mysterious things happen. But few of these tales have as much real evidence supporting them as the story of the ghostly faces on the S.S. *Watertown.*

The S.S. *Watertown* was a large oil tanker owned by a company called Cities Service. In December, 1924, the ship was on its way to the Panama Canal from the Pacific Ocean. Two seamen, James Courtney and Michael Meehan, were cleaning an empty oil tank on the ship. Unfortunately, gas fumes in the tank overcame them, and they died. They were buried at sea on December 4, 1924.

It was the next day that the ghostly faces ap-

An engraving of the ghostly ship *The Flying Dutchman,* by Gustave Doré

55

peared. The first mate and the men on his watch saw two faces following in the wake of the ship. He called the captain, Keith Tracy, to come up on deck to see them.

By this time the entire crew was up on deck looking at the faces. They were so clear that everybody saw them. Beyond a doubt in anybody's mind, the faces were those of the two dead men.

And the faces came back. They appeared for a few minutes day after day as the ship sailed slowly toward the canal. The ship traveled through the canal and into the Atlantic. It finally docked at its home port of New Orleans.

The captain gave a full report of what had happened to Cities Service. An official of the company, J. S. Patton, suggested that they try to photograph the faces. They decided to use the first mate's camera. Patton gave a sealed roll of film to the captain, who loaded the camera while the first mate watched.

The *Watertown* set sail for its return voyage to the Pacific. On the voyage the ghostly faces appeared again. Again the entire crew saw them. The faces always appeared in the same place. They remained visible for a few minutes and then faded from view.

During one of these appearances six snapshots

were taken of the two faces. The film was kept in the camera until the ship returned again to New Orleans. The film was then delivered to J. S. Patton, who sent it out to be developed. Five of the photographs showed only the railing of the ship. But the sixth photograph hit the jackpot. It clearly showed the two faces of the dead men projected on the water which followed the ship.

The whole story was reported in a company magazine of Cities Service. The magazine, called *Service,* carried the article in 1934.

More than ten years afterward the story was checked into by a man named Hereward Carrington. Carrington was experienced at finding out about ghostly happenings. He first tried to get interviews with the people who had been on the ship. But Patton and the first mate had died, and the captain and most of the crew had long since left the service. They could not be located.

Carrington did interview the manager of the company's New York office, Mr. Storey. Mr. Storey told him that at one time the New York office had publicly displayed a large blowup of the ghost photo. But the photographer who developed the film could not be traced, and no record had been kept.

Carrington did find out some facts about the appearance of the faces. It seems that the ghostly faces only appeared once in a while. They would stay for a few minutes and then fade out. The faces were always the same size. They would always appear at the same distance from the ship and in the same position.

The next attempt to check into the story was made in 1957. In that year a magazine called *Fate* ran an account of the story but without the photograph. It seems that the magazine could not find anyone who had the photo.

A reporter named Michael Mann read the article in the magazine and became very interested. He spent five years tracing the photo and finally tracked it down. Mann found out that the photos had been taken and sworn to by Captain Tracy and an engineer on the ship, Monroe Atkins. He also found out that the film had been checked for fakery by the Burns Detective Agency and found to be genuine. The negatives had been returned and had become the property of the ship's owners.

When Mann viewed the sixth photo, he could see that the faces were exactly as the witnesses had described them.

What do you think? The faces are clearly shown in the photo. Could they be a trick of the light or of the sea? Were the faces really those of the dead men? Were all the witnesses mistaken, or upset because of their friends' deaths?

It seems that after a while the sailors stopped seeing the faces. But they still believed that they had seen them. That's the way the story rests today. There remains one photograph of two faces on the waters of the sea and the stories of a host of witnesses.

THE HOUNDS OF DEATH

Stories about ghostly dogs are common in many countries. The British Isles in particular have more than their share of phantom dogs. The dogs often are seen just before or just after some terrible happening, usually a death.

One early story takes place in the English town of Tring, in the county of Hertford. It is said that an old woman was drowned there in 1751 for being a witch. The chimney sweep who drowned her was himself hanged in chains near the scene of the crime. From that time onward a large black dog haunted the place.

A century later an eyewitness account of the dog was published in the *Book of Days*. "I was returning late at night in a gig with the person who was driving. When we came near the spot . . . he saw on the bank of the roadside a flame of fire as large as a man's hat. . . . I then saw an immense black dog just in front of our horse. . . . He was as big as a New-foundland, but very gaunt, shaggy, with long ears and tail, eyes like balls of fire, and large, long teeth, for he opened his mouth and seemed to grin at us. In a few minutes the dog disappeared, seeming to vanish like a shadow. . . ."

There are many similar legends. In a book titled *The Norfolk Broadland,* the author, W. A. Dutt, de-scribes a ghostly hound called "Black Shuck." The word "Shuck" comes from an early Anglo-Saxon word for the devil. Dutt writes: "One of the most impressive phantoms, and one of the best known in Norfolk, is Old Shuck, a demon dog, as big as a fair-sized calf, that pads along noiselessly under the shadow of the hedgerows, tracking the steps of lone-ly wayfarers, and terrifying them with the wicked glare of his yellow eyes. To meet him means death within the year to the unhappy beholder."

In a more recent book titled *Day of Our Years,* Pierre Van Paasen tells a story of a ghostly dog he met in France. One evening a big black dog brushed past him. Van Paasen describes himself as feeling a chill such as one feels when ghosts are near. This happened in a house where the windows and doors were closed, and there was no other exit. But when

Van Paasen went looking for the dog, it was no-where to be found.

Van Paasen saw the dog several times again. After a while he began to worry that people would think him crazy, so he asked a friend and the friend's husky son to come and keep watch with him. The dog appeared to all of them. Not only that, it wagged its tail when they whistled at it. But when they came closer, it faded into thin air.

They finally decided to bring in two police dogs to keep watch. When the ghostly black dog appeared, the police dogs went wild with terror. One of them seemed to be fighting with an invisible foe. Then it dropped dead.

A famous ghost hunter named Elliott O'Donnel writes of some other terrifying hounds. O'Donnel collected many stories in England of hauntings by blue dogs, and sometimes blue dogs without heads. These ghost dogs were supposed to stay around very old cemeteries.

Here are two stories of these headless dogs. The first tale takes place in a house in Norfolk. A woman was awakened one night by something scratching on her windowpane high off the ground. She got out of bed to see what it was. There, pressed against the

glass, was the huge form of a shaggy dog without a head. It left without anything more happening.

The second story is even more terrifying. It seems a Mrs. du Barry was living in a house with her young son Philip and a few servants. Her husband had been ordered to go to India and was not present in the house.

The hauntings began soon after Mr. du Barry left. All the people in the house heard strange noises, scratchings, and whinings. The servants complained that when they were taking their meals, they felt that something they could not see would come sniffing around them. Sometimes the invisible thing would jump up on them. They would feel paws on their laps.

Much the same thing happened when they went to bed. The ghostly thing entered their rooms, sniffed around, and would leap into their beds with them. The servants were terrified and said that they would leave the house if the hauntings didn't stop.

Mrs. du Barry didn't know what to do. She tried to calm the servants' fears, but she had heard many of the same noises herself. Her final decision was brought about by what happened to her son, Philip.

One afternoon Philip was napping in his room.

Suddenly his mother heard him start to cry. Mrs. du Barry raced up the stairs and collided with Philip's governess. The governess was just coming out of Philip's room. Her eyes were bulging with terror, and her face was white as a sheet. She said not a word to Mrs. du Barry but just ran down the stairs and into the garden.

Dreading to think what had happened, Mrs. du Barry burst into the room. Philip was standing on his bed, beating at the air around him with his hands. "Take it away, take it away," he cried. "It is a horrid dog; it has no head!" Then, seeing his mother, Philip sprang down from the bed and raced into her arms. At the same instant something darted past Mrs. du Barry and disappeared through the open door. She saw it plainly. It was a huge greyhound without a head.

Mrs. du Barry left the house with her son the next day. But she hadn't seen the last of the ghostly dog. She related that the dog followed her and her son wherever they moved. It followed them till Philip's death, in Egypt, at the age of twenty-one. That certainly sounds like an example of a dog's loyalty that no one needs!

HAUNTED AMERICAN HISTORY

There are many stories of ghosts in America's past. Some are famous ghosts. Some are not so famous. But a ghostly history of the United States could easily fill several books. Here are just a few of these tales.

We'll begin in the home of presidents, the White House. A number of famous ghosts are supposed to be living there. One is Abigail Adams, wife of John Adams, who was the second president. She seems to be a busy ghost. During the presidency of William Howard Taft she was often seen passing through locked doors. It is said that she is still seen every so often hurrying down the halls.

Dolley Madison, wife of James Madison, has been seen a few times. Her most famous appearance came during the presidency of Woodrow Wilson. Mrs. Wilson had ordered the gardeners to move the rose garden Dolley had planted. Dolley was supposed to have come up to the gardeners. She told them in no uncertain terms to leave her roses alone. They stopped working at once. Today Dolley's garden remains exactly where she planted it.

There are some ghosts in the White House that don't seem to have names. Several people who have worked in the White House have written about them. Sometimes there are cold winds that shouldn't be there. Other times there are noises or loud laughter from empty rooms.

Certainly the most famous ghost in the White House is that of Abraham Lincoln. His ghost has been reported many times by different people. When he was president, he often stood looking out a window in the Oval Room. Since his death many employees of the White House have seen his figure standing at the window. Mrs. Calvin Coolidge was said to have seen him there also.

Queen Wilhelmina of the Netherlands was once a guest at the White House during the presidency of Franklin D. Roosevelt. There came a knock on her door one night. When she opened the door, she saw the ghost of Lincoln standing there. She told this story the next morning to President Roosevelt. He said he was not surprised. His wife, Eleanor, had also seen the ghost.

Though not set in the White House, there is another ghostly legend about Lincoln. It is said that on certain days in April two ghost trains appear on a track somewhere in the country. Both trains are pulled by old-time steam engines, with wide smokestacks and polished brass boilers.

The entire length of both trains is draped in black crape. The first train carries a large band playing funeral music. The second train has only a single flatcar following the engine. On the flatcar rests the lonely coffin of Abraham Lincoln.

Indians are a large part of the ghostly history of our country. They often seem to come back because of the shameful way they and their people have been treated. One story is about a Cherokee Indian named Tsali. Tsali's ghost has been seen now for more than one hundred years.

Tsali was a brave when the Cherokee nation stretched from the Great Smoky Mountains of Tennessee to the territory of Oklahoma. As white settlers came from the east, the Cherokees were pushed farther west. Wars were fought, and then treaties were signed. Much of the Cherokee land was taken away.

The final blow came when gold was discovered on

Cherokee land. Old treaties were forgotten, and a new treaty was signed in 1817. The Cherokees were to be moved from the Great Smoky Mountains to Oklahoma.

But it wasn't until 1838 that the army got around to enforcing the treaty. General Winfield Scott marched into Cherokee lands at the head of an army. The Cherokees had to move west within the month.

The soldiers built stockades and began rounding up Indians. Families were seized, many without their belongings. Their cattle were shot. Resisting Indians were beaten or killed. The forced marches to the West began.

It was wintertime when the Indians reached the banks of the Mississippi. They had no blankets or shelter. The soldiers didn't care. Thousands of Indians died before they reached Oklahoma. The harsh treatment of these Indians remains a terrible stain on American history.

Tsali was one of the Indians who was seized and sent to a stockade. But he and his family attacked their guards. They fled into the high mountains. But General Scott was determined not to let any resisting Indian go free.

Scott called in a trader. He told him to go into the

mountains with a message for Tsali. The message was to tell Tsali that if he came down and surrendered, the rest of his people could stay in the mountains.

Tsali accepted the offer. He came down from the mountains. Scott kept his word and left the other Indians alone. But he ordered that Tsali should be shot by a firing squad.

Since that time there have been many reports of Tsali's ghost. It usually appears in the autumn around harvest time. In the mist-covered peaks and valleys of the Great Smokies people swear they see the ghostly figure of an Indian. Outlined against the moon, they see Tsali moving proudly among the leafy trails of his home.

The time just before and during the Revolutionary War seems full of stories of headless ghosts. One of these tales is about the Battle of Fort Niagara. This was in 1759, twenty years before the Revolution.

Fort Niagara is on a little finger of land that is surrounded by water. The British troops had cut off the fort from the mainland. Inside the fort the French and Indians were under siege for two weeks. Life was very hard in the fort. Hot tempers were easily aroused. There were many quarrels.

Fort Niagara

During the siege two French officers had fallen in love with the same girl. They argued with each other every day. They finally decided to settle their differences with a duel. They met early one morning in the central courtyard of the fort.

They faced each other and drew their sharp steel sabers. But one of the officers was a much better swordsman than the other. Step by step he forced his enemy back. The end came suddenly. The sharp edge of a saber cut through flesh and bone. A head bounced on the cobbled pavement. Then there was a splash as the headless body fell into an open well in the courtyard.

We do not know what happened to the winner of the duel. But the headless ghost of the loser has been seen often. It walks the battlements of Fort Niagara. Rising out of the well at midnight, it searches all over for its long-lost head.

Washington Irving's story of Ichabod Crane and the Headless Horseman is the most famous headless ghost tale of the Revolution. But there are many other stories of headless galloping ghosts. In the middle of the war two British officers saw such a ghost. It was in Philadelphia, in Allen's Lane. One of their own soldiers came riding down the street, carrying his head before him on his saddle.

An engraving of Ichabod Crane pursued by the Headless Horseman

From a later period in our history comes a story of ghosts just before the Civil War. In those times many people in the North tried to help slaves escape from the South to Canada. Their escape route was called the Underground Railroad.

One of the way stations on the Underground Railroad was a house in Emmons, a small town in New York State. A tunnel led from a nearby river to the house. Escaping slaves coming up the river by boat used the tunnel. But the tunnel had been hastily dug. In some places the crumbling clay walls were held up by wooden sticks.

It was springtime, and there was much rain. Five or six black slaves had just arrived. They were crawling through the tunnel when the water-weakened walls collapsed. Their cries could be heard at both ends of the tunnel. Attempts were made to dig to them. But it was too late.

The spring rains still come to the town of Emmons. And sometimes in the rainy night cries are still heard. They sound like the voices of people trapped beneath the ground. The slaves had come so far in their battle for liberty. They seem to want to continue their journey.

Stories about ghosts are very much like ghosts

themselves. In the bright light of the sun, they seem silly and unreal. But then the sun sets and darkness falls. Shadows seem to twist in strange ways. Unexplained noises are all about. A little chill in the air makes us shiver. And suddenly ghost stories seem not so silly after all.

INDEX

77

About the Author

SEYMOUR SIMON was born in New York City, received his B.A. degree from City College, New York, and did graduate work there. He is the author of dozens of highly acclaimed science books on many subjects for young readers. A science teacher since 1955, he currently teaches at the Hawthorne Intermediate School, Long Island. Mr. Simon lives with his wife and two sons in Great Neck, New York.